My first
Communion
a day to remember

by Nadia Bonaldo

Pauline BOOKS & MEDIA

Nihil Obstat:
Very Rev. Timothy J. Shea, V.F.

Imprimatur:
✠Bernard Cardinal Law
September 21, 1993

Illustrations by Carla Cortesi

Artwork by N. Musio, pages 27, 31, 39, 41, 43, 47, 49, 72-73

Photo Credits:
Sr. Mary Emmanuel Alves, fsp—13, 15, 37, 45, 65, 77, 93, 99
Suzette Scherer—63, 69, 101
James Cryan—20-21
Daughters of St. Paul—35, 85, 87
Media Center—59
David S. Stickler—51

Graphic design by M. L. Benigni
Cover Design by Sergia Ballini, fsp

Original title: *La mia prima Comunione: Un giorno da ricordare.*
Copyright © 1991, Figlie di San Paolo, Milan, Italy.

Translated from the Italian by Janet and Frank Alampi
Edited by Mary James Berger, fsp

ISBN 0-8198-4770-4

Printed and published in the U.S.A. by Pauline Books & Media, 50 St. Paul's Avenue,
Boston, MA 02130.

Pauline Books & Media is the publishing house of the Daughters of St. Paul,
an international congregation of women religious serving the Church with
the communications media.

2   3   4   5   6   7   8   9   99   98   97   96   95

Contents

To _____

_____

_____

on the day of your First Communion Celebration. May Jesus be your best Friend now and forever.

Best wishes _____

_____

_____

_____

_____

On Sunday _____

at _____

in the parish of _____

I participated in my First Communion Liturgy.

photograph of my
first Communion Mass

For the first time
I have eaten the Host.
It is the **BODY** of **JESUS**.
And I drank from the chalice.
It is the **BLOOD** of **JESUS**.

The Risen Jesus
lives within me.
He and I are one.

I say **"THANK YOU"**
for the greatest gift
God has given me.

This is how I began
my adventure as
a child of God

A small seed...

When I was very small, my parents, godparents and many relatives and friends brought me to church.
I was baptized there.
I could not walk so they brought me.
I could not understand or talk.
So they understood and talked for me.

That day I became a child of God.
I became a member of a great family: the Church.

My parents and godparents
made a promise to God and the Church.
They promised to help me live and grow
as a child of God.

I was baptized at _____

on _____

I was given the name _____

which means _____

_____

_____

_____

_____

The name of the priest (or other minister)

who baptized me is

_____

_____

My godparents are

_____

_____

God our Father,
with Baptism
you have freed us from sin.
You have called us into your Church.
You have made us your children.
The Spirit of Jesus
lives in our hearts.

...Grows so slowly

This year I will be _____ years old.
I'm growing up.
There are always new things to learn.

I know now that at home I can't always say
"I want, I want."
I learn to think of how others feel.
Sometimes my daddy worries.
My mom works hard.
My little sister wants to play.
I learn to think of them, too.

At school I can't only think of doing better than the others.
Sometimes Tony is by himself.
Sometimes Nicole doesn't have a snack.
I learn to be kind to them.

I play with my friends.
I learn to take turns choosing games to play.
I learn not to be bossy.
I learn to share toys, even new ones.

This year Jesus is asking more of me.
He invites me to become his good friend.
He wants me to be very close to him.

Jesus says:
"I am the true vine, and my Father is the gardener....
Stay joined to me, and I will stay joined to you.
Just as a branch cannot produce fruit
unless it stays joined to the vine,
you cannot produce fruit
unless you stay joined to me.
I am the vine,
and you are the branches.
If you stay joined to me, and I stay joined to you,
then you will produce lots of fruit.
But you cannot do anything without me."

—*From the Gospel of St. John, chapter 15*
(John 15:1, 4-5, CEV)

An important choice

My parents and I have accepted Jesus' invitation. It was an important decision.

I don't understand everything that "making First Communion" means.
But I know two things for sure:

* I keep the promise my parents and godparents made for me when I was baptized.

* I answer Jesus' invitation to be his friend. He asks me to love just as he loves.

For now, I tell Jesus that I'm happy to know him better. I'm happy to listen to his Word and to do what he tells me.

I can use this prayer.

*I thank you, Lord, because you teach me your way.
"Obeying your instructions
brings as much happiness as being rich.
I will study your teachings
and follow your footsteps....
Your teachings are wonderful,
and I respect them all.
Understanding your word
brings light to the minds of ordinary people."*

—From Psalm 119
(Psalm 119:14-15, 129-130, CEV)

14

We are happy to be together as brothers and sisters

I've gone to religion class with other children. We have prepared ourselves for our First Communion.

Together we have learned that God loves us very much. We have found out about a great friend named Jesus.

THESE ARE MY FRIENDS FROM RELIGION CLASS

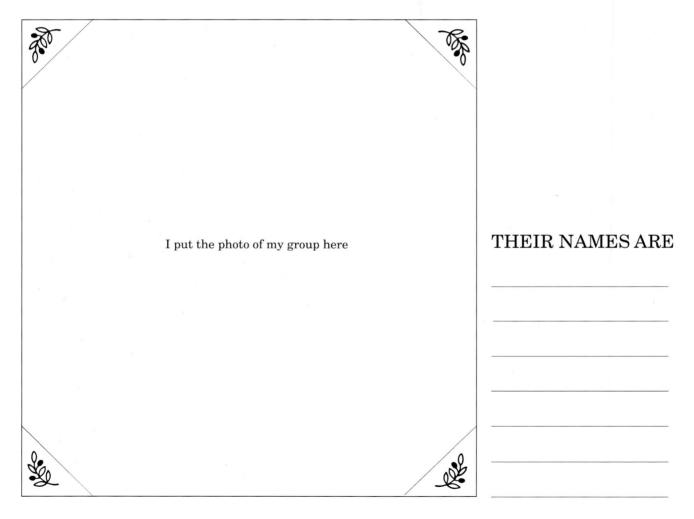

I put the photo of my group here

THEIR NAMES ARE

_____

_____

_____

_____

_____

_____

My teachers' names are

_____

What they do

_____

They decided to teach religion class because

_____

We met every _____

at this time _____

in this place _____

I pray for my religion teachers.

_____

_____

_____

I pray for my friends from religion class.

_____

_____

_____

The signs
of God's love

A rainbow...

I have learned many beautiful things during these months.
Above all, that God loves us very much.
God has always tried to be our friend.

Many, many years ago, for example....

God said to Noah:
"I am making a 'pact' with you
and your sons.
I promise never again
to send a flood
to destroy the earth.
I am putting a rainbow in the clouds.
It will be a sign of my promise.

**Whenever the RAINBOW appears,
I will remember my promise to you...."**

—From the Book of Genesis, chapter 9

...to remember

*The sign of the rainbow is
to remember a friendship.*

*Every time the people of Israel
see the rainbow in the sky
they will think of their friendship
with God.*

An adventure...

God has not only spoken through nature.
He came to his people wherever they were.
When people suffered he proved he was a friend.

This is how things happened many years later.

The people God loved were slaves of the Egyptians.
The people's lives had become terrible
because of the hard labor.
So they prayed to God, the friend of their fathers.
They asked him to remember them.

And so God decided to free his people.
He planned to bring them to a land rich and fertile.

He called Moses to be the leader of the Hebrew people.
God helped him lead the people across the Red Sea.
It was a great event, a real miracle.
The people were weak and defenseless.
Instead the Egyptians were rich and powerful.

Along the way they had many problems.
Moses encouraged them by saying;
"It is I who give the orders.
But it is God who leads us.
We have to trust him."

...to recount

To celebrate their freedom,
Moses and the Israelites sang to God.

"I will sing to the Lord.
He has won a great victory.
He has thrown horses
and riders into the sea.

The Lord is strong.
He helps me.
He has saved me.
I praise him, my God.

Who can do wonderful things
like you, Lord?
You keep your promises.

You are king forever."

—From the Book of Exodus, chapter 15

23

A lamb...

We like to remember wonderful adventures.
We especially like it when we are with friends.

The Hebrew people could not forget how they were freed
from slavery in Egypt.
They wanted to remember what God had done for them.
So every year the Hebrews ate a lamb.

This is how they celebrated Passover. God himself told
them to do this:

"Keep this day as a feast.
On this day I led you out of Egypt.
You must celebrate this feast forever."

—From the Book of Exodus, chapter 12

...to celebrate freedom

Here are the words the people of Israel use on the night
of Passover. They celebrate and thank God for creation,
freedom and the gift of his law.

"Praise the Lord for he is good!
God's love is everlasting.

Only God can work great wonders.
God's love is everlasting.

He made the sun and the moon.
God's love is everlasting.

God led his people out of Egypt.
God's love is everlasting.

God divided the Red Sea in two.
God's love is everlasting.

God brought Israel safely through the sea.
God's love is everlasting.

The Lord cast Pharaoh and his soldiers into the sea.
God's love is everlasting.

The Lord guided his people through the desert.
God's love is everlasting.

God remembered us when we were in trouble.
God's love is everlasting.

Praise God in heaven!
God's love is everlasting."

—*From Psalm 136*

But Jesus is the greatest gift

Later the people forgot all that God had done for them. They still did not love one another.

God sent a gift that was much more important than the rainbow.
This gift was much greater than freedom from Egypt.
God gave us himself.
God gave us his Son Jesus whom he loves very much.

It is important to know the life of Jesus.
It is important to learn about his words, his miracles, his death and resurrection.
If we want to know God we must look at Jesus.

Jesus has freed us from sin.
He helps us love each other as brothers and sisters.
His name "Jesus" means **"GOD SAVES."**
God could not give us a greater gift.

Jesus
the son of God
and the friend of all

The words of Jesus

Jesus lived in Nazareth, a small village in Galilee. He worked as a carpenter like his father Joseph. When Jesus was about thirty years old, he left his home and his work. He said good-bye to Mary his mother. He went from town to town. He had to tell everyone that God is a good Father. He told us that we must love one another. He wants us to be one, as he and the Father are.

Jesus walked along the white, dusty roads of Palestine. He spoke to the young and old. He spoke to people who lived good lives and to people who didn't. All the people were speechless as they listened to him. His words were not hard to understand. Everyone understood because Jesus' words touched their hearts.

One day Jesus climbed a high mountain. He spoke to the people. He said:

"God blesses those who put their trust in him.
God blesses those who are sad.
God blesses those who are not violent.
God blesses those who are kind to others.
God blesses those who are pure of heart.
God blesses those who are peacemakers.
God blesses those who suffer for doing what is right.

Be joyful and happy because God has prepared a great reward for you!"

—From the Gospel of Matthew, chapter 5
(Matthew 5:3-10, 12, CEV)

Jesus said,
Jesus said, "Let the children come to me,
and don't try to stop them!
People who are like these children
belong to God's kingdom."

—From the Gospel of Matthew, chapter 19
(Matthew 19:14, CEV)

And he went on to say

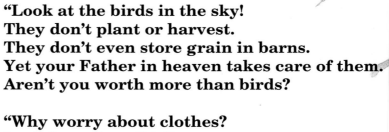

"Look at the birds in the sky!
They don't plant or harvest.
They don't even store grain in barns.
Yet your Father in heaven takes care of them.
Aren't you worth more than birds?

"Why worry about clothes?
Look how the wild flowers grow.
They don't work hard to make their clothes.
But I tell you that Solomon with all his wealth
was not as well clothed as one of them....

"Your Father in heaven knows that you need all of
these. But more than anything else,
put God's work first and do what he wants.
Then all other things will be yours as well."

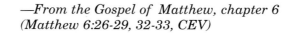

—From the Gospel of Matthew, chapter 6
(Matthew 6:26-29, 32-33, CEV)

"I am giving you a new command.
 You must love each other,
just as I have loved you.
If you love each other,
everyone will know that you are my disciples."

—From the Gospel of John, chapter 13
(John 13:34-35, CEV)

"Treat others as you want them to treat you."

—From the Gospel of Matthew, chapter 7
(Matthew 7:12, CEV)

"If you ask me for something in my name,
I will do it.
I will be with you forever,
all days,
until the end of the world."

The parables of Jesus

To tell everyone that God is a good Father, Jesus also spoke in parables. Parables are stories. Jesus used stories from the everyday life of the people of his time.

The parable of the lost sheep

Everyone loved Jesus very much. But there were also people who complained about Jesus. They complained about him because he spent time with sinners. Jesus knew very well what these complainers thought. One day he said to them:

"If one of you has a hundred sheep and loses one, what does he do? He leaves the ninety-nine safely in a sheep pen. Then he goes to look for the one that is lost until he finds it.
When he finds it, he is very happy. He puts it on his shoulder and returns home.
'Come to my house, come and we will celebrate,' he shouts to his friends and neighbors.
'I have found the sheep that was lost!'"

At the end of the story Jesus said: "God loves each one of us just like that shepherd. He knows each one of us. He takes care of us. He has no peace if even one is lost. I tell you that in heaven there is more happiness over one sinner who comes back to God than over the ninety-nine good people who don't need to."

—From the Gospel of Luke, chapter 15

"I am the good shepherd,"
says Jesus.
"I know my sheep,
and they know me.
I am ready to give
my life for my sheep."

The miracles of Jesus

Jesus didn't only tell beautiful stories and show love to everyone. He also worked many miracles. This is how he showed his power.

Jesus heals a little girl

One day, Jesus was walking. A man named Jairus fell at Jesus' feet. He was the leader of the synagogue (the place where the Hebrews went to pray). Jairus begged Jesus to go to his house. Jairus' only child, who was about twelve years old, was dying.

As they were going toward the house, Jairus' servant came toward them. He said, "Your daughter is dead. Don't bother the Master any more."

But Jesus said to the leader of the synagogue, "Don't be afraid. Only trust, and your daughter will be saved."

When Jesus reached Jairus' house, he found a great crowd of relatives and friends. They were all crying. When he heard all the noise, Jesus said, "Why are you crying and making all this noise? The child is not dead but asleep."

But no one believed him. They laughed at him.

So Jesus called the girl's parents and Peter, James and John. They went into the child's room with Jesus. Jesus knelt near her bed. He held the girl's hand. It was cold. Jesus said to her, "Little girl, get up!"

The little girl opened her eyes. In a flash, all smiles, she got up. Next Jesus told her parents to give her something to eat. He said not to let anyone know what had happened.

—From the Gospel of Luke, chapter 8

"Little girl, get up!" Jesus said to her.
The little girl opened her eyes and got up.

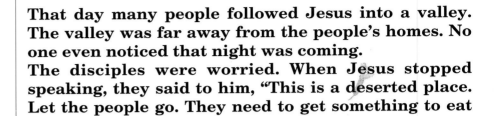

That day many people followed Jesus into a valley. The valley was far away from the people's homes. No one even noticed that night was coming.

The disciples were worried. When Jesus stopped speaking, they said to him, "This is a deserted place. Let the people go. They need to get something to eat before it gets dark."

Jesus answered, "Why don't you give them something to eat?"

The disciples were surprised. They looked at one another. Even King Herod's treasure would not be enough to feed all those people!

Then Andrew, Peter's brother, said jokingly, "There is a little boy here. He has five loaves of barley bread and two fish.... We can give a crumb to each person!..."

"Tell the people to sit down on the grass," Jesus told the disciples.

They saw that he was not joking.

Jesus took the five loaves and two fish. He said the blessing. Then he broke them and gave them to his disciples. They gave the food to the people. On that day all the people ate until they were satisfied.

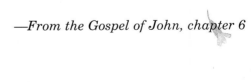

—*From the Gospel of John, chapter 6*

That strange story of the "living bread"

The next day the crowd that followed Jesus was even bigger. They thought that after his speech there would be another free meal.

But Jesus said, "You look for me because you have eaten the bread. But I will not give you anything to eat except myself. I am the living bread that comes from heaven. I am the bread that gives life. Those who believe in me will not be hungry any more. Those who trust me will not be thirsty any more."

They all looked at one another in surprise. "What is he saying? Has the sun gotten to him? Has he gone crazy during the night? Maybe we haven't really understood him!"

Jesus said, "If you do not eat my body and drink my blood, you will not have life in you! Those who eat my flesh and drink my blood are one with me and I with them. They will live forever."

"Now he is making this up! Who can listen to things like this? How can he give us his body to eat?" And even those who had been following Jesus for a long time went away.

Only the Twelve stayed. They were hurt and disappointed.

"Do you want to leave, too?" Jesus asked. He looked into their eyes.

But Peter said, "Lord, to whom shall we go? Only you speak the words that give eternal life!"

So the Twelve stayed with him.

The story of the "living bread" seemed to end there.

—from the Gospel of John, chapter 6

"Do you want to leave, too?"
Jesus asked.
"Lord, to whom shall we go?
Only you speak the words that give life!"
So the Twelve stayed with him.

The last supper explains everything

Passover was near. On this day, the Hebrews celebrated their freedom from slavery in Egypt. They renewed their pact of friendship with God. Jerusalem was full of people. They came from all over.

The Apostles also prepared everything for the feast. There was a lamb, some wine, and some bread. Jesus knew that this would be his last supper with his friends.

During the supper Jesus took the bread. He broke it and gave it to his friends. He said,
"Take this. It is my body which is given for you."
And he gave it to them to eat.
Then he took the cup of wine. He said,
"This is my blood given for you. Do this in memory of me."
Then he gave it to them to drink.

And so, they understood better the speech about the living bread.

*Jesus
loves us so much
that he gave
his life for us.*

43

He loved his friends to the end

Jesus' Passover meal with his friends was over. They went to a garden called Gethsemane. It was close by and Jesus often rested there with his disciples.

Things started to happen very quickly. The garden was suddenly filled with noises. Lanterns shone in the darkness. Men carrying weapons came toward Jesus. For a long time they had waited to capture him and put him to death. The moment had arrived. Thursday night and Friday were also terrible for Jesus' disciples.
When their Master died, their hopes died, too. They did not understand that he died to give us life. They did not understand that he would rise. They were afraid. So much had happened in such a short time! They locked themselves in a house. All day Saturday they stayed there. They cried for Jesus, their friend who had died.

"The greatest way to show love for friends is to give your life for them," said Jesus.

The life of Jesus was like bread.
He gave it to all those whom he met.
He had "broken" himself for everyone.
He never thought of himself.

The life of Jesus was like bread and wine.
He "broke" himself for everyone.
He "poured" himself out for everyone.
He never thought of himself.

Jesus is alive

On Sunday morning Mary of Magdala went to the tomb where they had put Jesus' body. Some other women went with her. They brought perfumes to anoint Jesus' body. This was a Jewish custom. The women did not speak along the way. They were worried. They wondered who would move the large stone in front of the tomb for them.

But when they arrived, the tomb was open. The rock was rolled far away. They saw that something special had happened.

When they went into the tomb, they heard a voice. "Why do you look here for someone who is no longer dead? Jesus is not here. He is risen, he is alive. Go and tell his friends!"

The women left the tomb in a hurry.
They were both afraid and happy.
They ran to tell the disciples,
"Jesus is risen!"

Forever with us

That day, Jesus himself appeared to the disciples. At first they thought he was a ghost. They had locked the door of the room where they were hiding because they were afraid. How could a living person get in?

"Peace be with you!" Jesus said. "Do not be afraid. Touch me and look at me. It is really I. A ghost cannot have flesh and bones like I do!"

Jesus' friends were happy to see him.

And Jesus said again, "Peace be with you. As the Father has sent me, so I send you." He breathed on them. Then he said, "Receive the Holy Spirit."

*Now it was as if
the disciples had a fire inside their hearts.
The Risen Jesus
had given them his Spirit.
They would never be alone.*

49

Sunday: the day of the Risen Lord

The disciples often talked about the day they had met the risen Jesus. They said, "It was on the day of the Lord." They called that day "Sunday."

So each Sunday the disciples would come together to break the bread and drink from the same cup." The Mass soon became the center of life for the first Christians. When they ate the bread and drank from the cup, they became one with the Risen Jesus. His friends were changed from frightened men into brave men. They faced suffering without fear. They began their journeys to the corners of the earth.

Sunday is a special day for us too.
Today the place where we go to pray is different.
The songs and the language are different, too.
But we, too, receive the Body and Blood of Jesus.
We meet the Risen Jesus.
It is just like we were with him on the banks of Lake Galilee.

51

Forgive us, Lord

The priest invites us to be silent. He invites us to ask pardon for all our sins. It's a little hard. I feel very excited. I know that this moment is important. I want to be able to welcome Jesus with a loving heart. I think of what I have done during the week.

I made up excuses for not helping my mother.
I made believe I didn't hear what my grandfather
asked me.
Lord, have mercy.

I was unkind to my classmates.
I didn't always listen to what my teacher said.
Christ, have mercy.

I didn't help my sister with her chores.
I left my toys around.
Lord, have mercy.

The priest prays. We pray with him that
God may have mercy on us.
We ask God to forgive us our sins.
We ask him to bring us to heaven with him.

It's wonderful to have a friend like you, Jesus.
You always forgive us.
You never get tired of loving us.
Not because we are good,
but because you are Love.

Glory to God

You have forgiven us, Lord.
We have many reasons for praising you today.
Glory to you, God the Father. You are good, you love us.
We all sing, young and old. We are one voice.
One family.
We feel like your children.

Holy Father, Creator of the world,
you rule the heavens and the earth.
We ask that your kingdom come,
that your will be done.

Jesus Christ, Lamb of God,
you take away the sins of the world.
You sit at the right hand of the Father.
Listen to our prayer.

Glory to you, Holy Spirit,
who unite the Church in one body.
You spread your gifts all over the world.
You are a fountain of life and love.

Glory to God
and peace to his people.
We adore you.
We give you thanks.
We praise you, Lord.

59

Speak, Lord,
we are listening

Everyone is quiet because now the Lord speaks. We don't
see him. But he speaks through the voice of that mother
(or father) who is reading from the big book of the Word of
God.
Jesus also speaks today, just as he spoke a long time ago to
the crowds in Palestine.

The Word of God is like a seed.
Our heart is the ground where it's planted.

Lord, for many, many years
your Word has been read
all over the world.
Your Word is always true.

Lord, your Word is a light for us.
It tells us all you have done.
It's like a lamp on our path.

Lord, your Word is not just any word.
Help me to do what your Word tells me.
To feel you close to me.
To feel like your friend.

I remember these words from the Word of God in my First Communion Mass:

_____

_____

I remember these words from the Gospel read by the priest:

_____

After the Gospel the priest explained the Word of God to us. This is what I remember:

_____

_____

_____

_____

_____

_____

_____

_____

"Happy are those who listen to the Word of God,"
says Jesus, "and live it every day."

We believe

We have listened to the Word of the Lord.
The priest has helped us to understand it. May it grow and bloom just like the seed planted in good soil. Now we are all invited to say what we believe. We say a prayer called the Creed. In many countries people can't talk about their faith in you, God. So I say with all my strength that I believe in you. I believe that you love us.

I believe in one God,
the Father,
Creator of heaven and earth.

I believe in Jesus Christ,
the only Son of God,
who died and is risen for us.

I believe in the Holy Spirit,
the Lord, the giver of life.

This is our faith.
This is the faith of the Church.

62

Hear us, O Lord

We really feel like brothers and sisters.
We are children of the same Father.
We are one family: the Church.
As in every family, each one has his or her duty.
Each one is important.
If one suffers, the others are also less happy.
If one is happy, the others are all happy, too.
This is how it is in the Church.
Now we pray for all the needs, wishes, and suffering of all
the people.

Let's pray

for the Church, the Pope, the bishops;
for priests, religious, missionaries,
for our families, for our religion teachers;
for the people who make our laws,
for everyone who takes care of us;
for children, for young and older adults;
for those who are alone, who are poor or sick;
for the hungry and for those in prison.

The prayer of one
becomes the prayer of all.
And we answer loudly:
Lord, hear our prayer.

...Jesus took the bread and wine...

Now as then

We all sit down.
Now the Liturgy of the Eucharist begins. The priest takes the bread and wine. He puts them on the altar.

There is a beautiful white tablecloth. It's like the one my mother uses for special occasions. We are also preparing a feast. A very special feast.

The bread we eat and the wine we drink feed us in a very special way. The priest thanks the Lord for these gifts.

Blessed are you, O Lord, who have created all things.
You have given us this bread that we offer to you.
It will become the bread of life for us.

Blessed be God forever.

We thank you also for this wine,
made of many grapes.
It will become our spiritual drink.

Blessed be God forever.

This bread is made of a thousand grains of wheat.
They have been ground up
and kneaded to make this bread.

This wine is made up of many grapes.
When we offer the bread and wine,
we offer ourselves, too.

It's as if each of us—
Mark, Ann, Larry, Marie—
were on the altar, like a gift.

We offer you, good Father,
our desire to play, to jump and run.
And today we also offer our desire
to be good friends of Jesus.
May we always walk with him.

We offer you, good Father,
the pains of those who suffer.
We offer you the worries of those
who have many problems.
We offer you the desires and hopes
of each person's heart.

...Jesus offered thanks...

Now as then

Everything is ready on the altar. It has become a beautiful table. The church is like the hall where Jesus ate the last supper with his friends. All this is possible because he is risen from death. He lives. By the power of the Holy Spirit, the bread and wine will become Jesus' Body and Blood. Now as then, Jesus gives his life for us.

The priest repeats the words and actions of Jesus. We pay attention to what he is saying and doing.

WE GIVE THANKS TO GOD THE CREATOR

O God our Father,
you have brought us together again.
We are here to say "thank you."
We want to sing your praise.
We praise you for all the great and wonderful
things you have made.
We thank you for the joy you put in our heart.
We bless you for the sun
which gives light to the day.
We bless you for your Word,
which is light for our mind.
We thank you for the fields,
for the oceans and the mountains.
We thank you for the people who live on earth.
We thank you for the life you have given us.
For all these wonderful gifts of your love
we sing your praise.

68

*Heaven and earth
are full of your glory.
Praise to you!*

We thank God the Father for the gift of Jesus

Good Father, you always watch over us.
You never forget anyone.
To free us from sin you sent your Son Jesus,
our Savior.
He lived with us and did good to everyone.
He healed the sick. He gave sight to the blind.
He pardoned sinners.
He welcomed children and blessed them.
O Father, in Jesus we see your great love
for everyone!
And now we show our joy in song.

**Blessed is he who comes
in the name of the Lord.
Praise to you!**

One people

Good Father,
we offer you our praise.
We praise you with your Church all over the world.
We praise you with our Pope and our bishop.
Together with your Mother Mary,
with the apostles,
with the angels and all the saints,
we sing the hymn
of your glory.

Holy, holy, holy, Lord...
Praise to you!

Holy Father,
to show our thanks
we have brought the
bread and wine to the altar.

Send your Holy Spirit upon these gifts,
that they may become
Jesus' Body and Blood.
In this way we can offer you
what you have given us as a gift.
A gift of your love.

71

Do this

At the last supper with his disciples,
Jesus took the bread.
He gave thanks.
He broke it and gave it to them. He said:

**Take this
all of you
and eat it.
This is my body
which will be
given for you.**

72

in memory of me

In the same way,
he took the cup of wine
He gave thanks.
He gave it to his disciples and said:

Take this
all of you
and drink from it.
This is the cup
of my blood.
It is the blood
of the new
and everlasting
covenant.
My blood will be
shed for you and
for everyone
so that sins may
be forgiven.

Then he said to
them:

*DO THIS
IN MEMORY
OF ME.*

73

We offer the Father the most pleasing gift: the life of Jesus

There is silence while the priest prays.
We all know something special is happening.
Once again, at this very moment, Jesus gives his life to God
the Father for all of us.

Now, Father,
we do what Jesus has told us.
We offer you the bread of life.
We offer you the cup of salvation.
We proclaim Jesus'
death and resurrection.

Jesus, you gave your life for me.
I too can offer my life to the Father, every day.
I can offer it with you.

I offer my wish to play.
I offer my wish to learn new things.
I offer _____

_____

_____

Christ has died for us.
Christ is risen for us.
Come, Lord Jesus.

We pray for the whole world

Father, you love us so much.
You let us receive
the Body and Blood of Jesus.
All together in the joy
of the Holy Spirit,
may we be one family.

Look with kindness on our parents,
our brothers and sisters,
and our friends,
on those who work,
on those who suffer,
on us who are here,
and on all the people of the world.

Lord, welcome those who have died
into the joy of heaven.
O Father,
we will always praise
and thank you for your great love.

Through Christ,
with Christ,
in Christ,

in the unity of the Holy Spirit,
all glory is yours, O Father,
forever and ever.

Amen.

Father of all

The bread and wine are now the **LIVING JESUS**.
He is here with us as he promised during the last supper.
This bread and this wine make us all brothers and sisters.
We are children of the same Father.
With joy we say:

Our Father, who art in heaven,
hallowed be thy name;

      O God may all people
      know that you are **FATHER.**

thy kingdom come;
thy will be done
on earth as it is in heaven.

      Your kingdom has come with Jesus.
      He has brought us peace, brotherhood and truth.
      But you ask each of us to help make the world
      a better place.

Give us this day
our daily bread;

      Everything is a gift from you, Father.
      I offer you my hands and my heart.
      Jesus is our bread, because Jesus is life.

and forgive us
our trespasses.

You never stop loving us, Father.
Each time you forgive us,
you give us even more love.

as we forgive those
who trespass against us;

Jesus, teach us to forgive as you forgive us.
I need to know how to forgive
so I can be your friend.

and lead us not
into temptation,

May we not give in to temptation.
Lead us.
Help us be strong so we can be good.

but deliver us from evil.

Free us from war and selfishness.
Give us real peace.
So we can all live happily
in the wonderful world you have created for us.

The peace of the Lord be with you

The Risen Jesus gave a great gift to his disciples.
He gave them his peace.
Now the priest offers us the same peace.

**The peace of the Lord
be with you always.**

We shake hands with those on our right and left.
I want to give a sign of peace to my whole family,
and to the whole world.
This comes from the peace of the Risen Jesus.

**Peace be with you, my sister.
Peace be with you, my brother.
Peace be with all the people
loved by the Lord.**

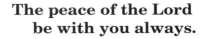

This is the commandment I give you.
Always love each other
as I have loved you.

The world will know
that you are my disciples
if you love one another.

I give you peace—
not as the world gives it.
Live always in my love.

...He broke the bread and gave it to them...

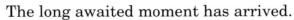

Now as then

The long awaited moment has arrived.
The bread and wine on the altar have become the Body and Blood of Jesus.
Now for the first time I will receive Jesus' Body and Blood.
This is why I have come here today with my family.

HAPPY ARE WE
WHO ARE INVITED
TO THE SUPPER OF
THE RISEN LORD!

"I am the bread, the living bread from heaven," says Jesus. "Those who eat this bread will live forever."

You come to me.
I come to you.
Together we celebrate
because...

You love me very much.
I love you very much.
Together we celebrate
because...

This is our day,
the day of our meeting,
and you love me, Lord.

You speak a little with me.
I speak a little with you.
Together this is very
beautiful because...

You really listen to me.
I really listen to you.
Together this is a joy
because...

This is our day,
the day of our meeting,
and you love me, Lord.

You stay here with me.
I stay here with you.
Together this is a joy
because...

You give me your hand.
I give you my hand.
Together this is a joy
because...

You are my best friend for life.
I will walk with you, Lord Jesus.

(A. M. Galliano, *Meeting with Jesus*)

83

The Body of Christ Amen!

This bread we eat was once a very small seed.
It was inside the darkness of the earth.
Then it became...a field of wheat.
Many stalks swayed in the wind.
Many grains were ground up.

Jesus, this bread was made from grain.
It grew in the sun.
It was made by the wind and by the fire.
It was made by many people with love.
Now it is your **BODY, LORD JESUS**.

From your hands we receive this bread we eat.
Jesus, may your Spirit join our hearts as one.
May we live in joy.
Thank you, Jesus.

The Blood of Christ
Amen!

This wine which we drink
began as a root in the earth.
Then it became...bunches of grapes.
They were harvested, then they were crushed.
Jesus, this wine was made of grapes.
They grew in the sun.
It was made by the wind and the weather.
It was made by many people with love.
Now it is your BLOOD, LORD JESUS.

From your hands
we receive this wine which we drink.
Jesus, may your Spirit
join our hearts as one.
May we live in joy.
Thank you, Jesus.

(A. M. Galliano, *One Fine Day*)

86

My first Communion

I eat the **BREAD.**
I drink the **WINE.**
The life of Jesus becomes my life.
The bread becomes my blood, skin, heart, energy, strength, and courage.
It is the life of the Risen Jesus.

Lord Jesus,
I believe you are the living bread.
Only you give me joy and peace.

I put the photo
of my first Communion here

We have eaten the Body of Jesus.
Everyone around us is quiet.
Each of us is thinking about God being with us.
He is living and strong, hidden in that small piece of bread.

This is what I said to Jesus when I made my
First Communion:

_____

_____

_____

_____

_____

_____

_____

_____

_____

_____

_____

Your Body will always be
the bread that gives me strength.
Your Body will make my steps safe.

Your Blood will always be
the wine that takes away my thirst.
Your Blood will give me the courage to follow you.

Let us go in peace

It's time to say good-bye.
The Lord gives us another gift: his blessing.
He is saying to each of us,
"Go in peace. I am always with you!"

GO IN PEACE
does not only mean that we may now go home.
No, it means that in all we do, we bring Jesus to others.

Every time I eat his bread which gives life,
Jesus makes me more like himself.

90

Lord, make me an instrument of your peace.
Where there is hatred, let me bring love.
Where there is injury, let me bring pardon.
Where there is doubt, let me bring faith.
Where there is despair, let me bring hope.
Where there is darkness, let me bring light.
Where there is sadness, let me bring joy.

St. Francis

We remain in love

My friends,
may the Lord's celebration
never end for you.
REMAIN IN LOVE
and God will be with you.

My friends,
may the Lord's joy
shine in you.
REMAIN IN LOVE
and God will be with you.

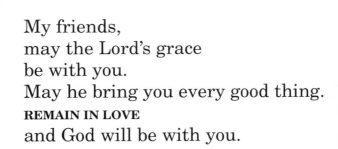

My friends,
may the Lord's grace
be with you.
May he bring you every good thing.
REMAIN IN LOVE
and God will be with you.

My friends,
may the Lord's strength
guide your steps.
REMAIN IN LOVE
and God will be with you.

(A. M. Galliano, *I Come to You*)

92

I put photos
of my family
here

"God is love.
If we keep on loving others, we will stay one in our hearts with God, and he will stay one with us."

—From the First Letter of John, chapter 4
(1 John 4:16, CEV)

A celebration
without end

A new strength

Many days have passed since my First Communion Mass.
Nothing seems to have changed.
I still go to school.
I do my homework. I play.
I still fight sometimes with my sisters and brothers.
My father and mother still work as they did before.

But everything is the same only on the outside.
Inside me there is a new strength.
It is the strength of the Lord Jesus.
His Spirit reminds us of what he said.

**Love one another.
By this they will know
that you are my disciples.**

It is not easy, Jesus, to love as you love.
But you promised not to leave us alone.
You will always be with us.
One day you will return.
Then we will see you face to face.
Meanwhile, you want us to love each other.
You want us to prepare for our most important
meeting with you.

I look around
and see you present

I see you, Lord Jesus,
in the love of my mother and father.
I see you in the patience of my grandparents.
I see you in the friendship of my friends.

I see you, Lord Jesus,
in all the people who work to make things better
in our world.
I see you in the people who help
the elderly, the sick,
the handicapped.

I see you, Lord Jesus,
in that family helping
a young person addicted to drugs.
I see you also in that family
that has adopted another child.

I see you present, Lord Jesus,
in the priests, religious and missionaries.
I see you in all those people who help others.

I also carry my small burden

Jesus, I want to help other people to know you. I want them to know you are close to them.

I can help my father and mother
by showing my love for them.

I can help my teacher
by obeying.

I can help my friends
to love one another more.
I can help them welcome new friends.

I can help other people
to smile.

Jesus, I am only a child.
But you need me, too,
to build a more beautiful world.
I could not do much by myself.
But with you I can.
I take part in Mass on Sunday
to listen to you,
to become one with you,
and to bring you to others.

My weekly Eucharist

The church where I go to Mass is called

_____

The children's Mass is at

_____

I go to Mass with

_____

_____

The part of Mass I like most is

_____

_____

The most beautiful words I hear during Mass are

_____

_____

The hardest words are

_____

_____

"Your kindness and love
will always be with me each day of my life,
and I will live forever in your house, Lord."

—*From Psalm 23*
(Psalm 23:6, CEV)

auline BOOKS & MEDIA

ALASKA
750 West 5th Ave., Anchorage, AK 99501   907-272-8183
CALIFORNIA
3908 Sepulveda Blvd., Culver City, CA 90230   310-397-8676
5945 Balboa Ave., San Diego, CA 92111   619-565-9181
46 Geary Street, San Francisco, CA 94108   415-781-5180
FLORIDA
145 S.W. 107th Ave., Miami, FL 33174   305-559-6715
HAWAII
1143 Bishop Street, Honolulu, HI 96813   808-521-2731
ILLINOIS
172 North Michigan Ave., Chicago, IL 60601   312-346-4228
LOUISIANA
4403 Veterans Memorial Blvd., Metairie, LA 70006   504-887-7631
MASSACHUSETTS
50 St. Paul's Ave., Jamaica Plain, Boston, MA 02130
  617-522-8911
Rte. 1, 885 Providence Hwy., Dedham, MA 02026   617-326-5385
MISSOURI
9804 Watson Rd., St. Louis, MO 63126   314-965-3512
NEW JERSEY
561 U.S. Route 1, Wick Plaza, Edison, NJ 08817   908-572-1200
NEW YORK
150 East 52nd Street, New York, NY 10022   212-754-1110
78 Fort Place, Staten Island, NY 10301   718-447-5071
OHIO
2105 Ontario Street (at Prospect Ave.), Cleveland, OH 44115
  610-621-9427
PENNSYLVANIA
Northeast Shopping Center, 9171-A Roosevelt Blvd. (between
Grant Ave. & Welsh Rd.), Philadelphia, PA 19114   215-676-9494
SOUTH CAROLINA
243 King Street, Charleston, SC 29401   803-577-0175
TENNESSEE
4811 Poplar Ave., Memphis, TN 38117   901-761-2987
TEXAS
114 Main Plaza, San Antonio, TX 78205   210-224-8101
VIRGINIA
1025 King Street, Alexandria, VA 22314   703-549-3806
GUAM
285 Farenholt Avenue, Suite 308, Tamuning, Guam 96911;
  671-649-4377
CANADA
3022 Dufferin Street, Toronto, Ontario, Canada M6B 3T5
  416-781-9131